Difficult to Discover,
Priceless in Value . . .

True

Friends Are Precious
Treasures.

To My True Friend: _____

From: _____

Date: _____

True Friends

Sentimental
REFLECTIONS

"Let the little children come to me, and do not hinder them,
for the kingdom of God belongs to such as these."

—Mark 10:14

True Friends

Featuring images by Sentimental Productions.

Artwork is reproduced under license from Sentimental Productions and may not be reproduced without permission. For information on other products featuring these charming photographs, contact:

Sentimental Productions
www.sentimentalproductions.com

For licensing information, contact Evergreen Ideas, Inc. (615) 826-6775.

Art ©2001 by Brad Lind
Text ©2001 by Alan Cox
Production by Leisha Lindstrom

Unless otherwise indicated, all Scripture quotations are taken from the *Holy Bible, New International Version*®. NIV®. Copyright © 1973, 1978, 1984 by International Bible Society. Used by permission of Zondervan Publishing House. All rights reserved.

This book produced by Sentimental Productions. Special thanks to Melissa Cox (for lovingly enduring the long road to reality for this project), Lynn Lind (for letting us invade your tidy home with tons of messy children), Greg Lindstrom (for being a true friend and soul-mate under fire), and Tim O'Hare (for pouring your time and talent into this project).

This edition published by Honor Books, P.O. Box 55388, Tulsa, Oklahoma 74155.

Printed and bound in China.

ISBN 1-56292-894-5

01 02 03 04 05 06 07 08 09 10/TK/10 9 8 7 6 5 4 3 2 1

Dedicated to our children, whom we cherish, adore, and hope to be True Friends with forevermore.

May the God of hope
fill you with
all joy and peace
as you trust in him.

—Romans 15:13

Reflections on Relationships

Introduction

There is a friend who sticks closer than a brother.

—Proverbs 18:24

Few things can measure up to the joy of authentic friendship. Having dedicated individuals cheer us through the highest highs and comfort us through the lowest lows makes the journey of daily living both meaningful and memorable.

Over the course of our lives, we interact with an overwhelming number of personalities. Some become acquaintances. A smaller number become friends. And a very special few can claim the title of *True Friends.*

True Friends are gifts from God who are meant to be cherished and preserved. We hope this book helps you do just that. Throughout these pages you'll be invited to reflect and record your memories shared with *True Friends,* both from your past (glancing back) and in the months and years to come (glimpsing ahead).

This book is a place to store your treasure—those timeless moments when your soul is stirred by the love and support of a *True Friend.* By capturing your memories on these pages, you'll gain a better appreciation for their tremendous value and a new perspective on life's truly priceless possessions.

There is mystery and wonder in the way God provides people to enrich our lives. He uses *True Friends,* despite their imperfections, to give us a glimpse of His perfect love. And that is worth taking note of . . . again and again.

Encouraging

giving hope
and confidence

During Those Times When Your Cup Feels Empty ...

True Friends

Fill Each Other Up with Support and Grace.

Therefore encourage one another and build each other up, just as in fact you are doing.
—1 Thessalonians 5:11

Encouraging: Glancing Back

W ords of encouragement are so powerful. They can literally give you strength and courage when you feel like giving up. Think back to the times in your life when you felt ready to throw in the towel. Who really showed themselves to be your *True Friends,* and how did they encourage you?

_____

_____

_____

_____

_____

_____

_____

_____

_____

_____

_____

_____

Encouraging: Glimpsing Ahead

Over the years, God will place special people in your life to cheer you on with kind words of support. He will also give you opportunities to be there when others need encouragement. Use this space to record ongoing instances when you are encouraged by a friend, as well as times when you are a *True Friend* to someone else.

_____

_____

_____

_____

_____

_____

_____

_____

_____

_____

_____

_____

Imparting

sharing lessons learned

Every Once
in a While,

When You Need a Little Advice . . .

True Friends

Share Their
Life Experiences
and Stories.

Whatever you have learned
or received or heard from me,
or seen in me—put it into practice.
And the God of peace will be with you.
                                    —Philippians 4:9

Imparting: Glancing Back

Hearing people share their life experiences can be hilarious, but it can also be very heart-warming. Vulnerability opens a window to the heart and gives us a glimpse of what can be learned from tough times. Think back to a few key times in your life when *True Friends* passed on the things they learned from experience. How did you benefit from their openness?

_____

_____

_____

_____

_____

_____

_____

_____

_____

_____

_____

Imparting: Glimpsing Ahead

Throughout life, you'll meet special people who will share their mistakes, trials, and disappointments—along with the lessons they learned in the process. You'll also find that God will put you in a position to be a *True Friend*. Use this space to write about the people who open their hearts to pass on wisdom, as well as instances when you share lessons God taught you with others.

_____

_____

_____

_____

_____

_____

_____

_____

_____

_____

_____

_____

Giving

being thoughtful and generous

At Those Special Moments When You Get a Taste of the Good Life . . .

True Friends Enjoy the Sweetness of Both Giving and Receiving.

"Freely you have received, freely give."
—Matthew 10:8

Giving: Glancing Back

Generosity is an outward expression of an inward condition—a grateful heart. Sometimes even the smallest acts of kindness can mean the world to others. Consider the times in your life when you benefited from people's willingness to give freely of their time, talent, or treasure. What sort of impact did it make?

_____

_____

_____

_____

_____

_____

_____

_____

_____

_____

_____

_____

_____

Giving: Glimpsing Ahead

Every so often in life, you will benefit from another's generosity. You'll also be presented with opportunities to help others. Use this space to write about the times *True Friends* touch you with their giving spirit, as well as times you do the same. Be sure to note how both of them made you feel.

_____

_____

_____

_____

_____

_____

_____

_____

_____

_____

_____

Serving

putting
others' needs
first

On Those Days
When It Seems
Like Every Man Is for Himself . . .

True Friends

Put Others' Needs before Their Own.

The Lord will reward everyone for whatever good he does.
—Ephesians 6:8

Serving: Glancing Back

Conventional wisdom suggests we're all in one great big competition and that you have to take care of your wants and needs first. That's what's so unconventional about *True Friends!* The only real competition between *True Friends* is about who can serve the other more. They don't keep score. Everybody wins. When have people put your needs above their own? How did their sacrifice strengthen and support you?

_____

_____

_____

_____

_____

_____

_____

_____

_____

_____

_____

_____

_____

_____

Serving: Glimpsing Ahead

It may defy logic, but it's "selflessness"—not selfishness—that leads to self-satisfaction. In your greatest times of need, your *True Friends* will make even greater sacrifices. Use this space to write about some of the incredible times when people put your desires, interests, and needs ahead of their own. Describe what makes it so meaningful. Then consider how you can serve others.

_____

_____

_____

_____

_____

_____

_____

_____

_____

_____

_____

_____

Believing In

being
confident in
someone

In the Moments When You Can't Fully Grasp Your Full Potential . . .

True Friends

See Each Other for All They Can Be.

However, as it is written:
"No eye has seen, no ear has heard,
no mind has conceived
what God has prepared for those
who love him."

—1 Corinthians 2:9

Believing In: Glancing Back

We sometimes fall victim to an unwelcome inner voice that drones doubtful statements like, "Why risk it; you'll probably just fail" and "Give up; you'll never make it." *True Friends* offer a positive point of view. They believe in us—even when we no longer do—and help us achieve more than we thought possible. Describe the times in your life when someone's confidence in you enabled you to accomplish something.

_____

_____

_____

_____

_____

_____

_____

_____

_____

_____

_____

_____

Believing In: Glimpsing Ahead

Self-doubt may show up at those times when just a little confidence would take you a very long way. Although you may question your abilities, *True Friends* remind you that Jesus is at work in you and through Him you can do all things. Use the space below to write about the times when their confidence makes a real difference in your life. Also, take note of the times when your belief in others helps them reach new heights.

_____

_____

_____

_____

_____

_____

_____

_____

_____

_____

_____

_____

Appreciating

disregarding others' shortcomings

Sometimes There's too Much Pressure to Be Perfect . . .

True Friends Value Attempts as Much as Results.

*My grace is
sufficient for you,
for my power
is made perfect
in weakness.*
—2 Corinthians 12:9

41

Appreciating: Glancing Back

For a guaranteed approach to experiencing disappointment, try expecting perfection. None of us have the ability to get it right every time, yet we frequently demand this from others. *True Friends* appreciate valiant attempts as much as victorious outcomes. When did someone make you feel appreciated for who you were, not what you did. How did it impact you?

_____

_____

_____

_____

_____

_____

_____

_____

_____

_____

_____

_____

Appreciating: Glimpsing Ahead

It's perfectly absurd to expect perfection, since we all fall short of the glory of God. In addition to the unnecessary pressure it places upon a friendship, it fortifies our fear of failure. *True Friends* are focussed on lifting each other up, not letting each other down. Use this space to write about the times *True Friends* make you feel appreciated, even when you've let them down.

_____

_____

_____

_____

_____

_____

_____

_____

_____

_____

_____

_____

Forgiving

granting
freedom from guilt

A fter a Few Angry Words, It's Easy to Feel Distant from the Ones You Love . . .

True Friends

Don't Let Disagreements Come between Them.

Be kind and compassionate to one another,
forgiving each other, just as in Christ God forgave you.
—Ephesians 4:32

Forgiving: Glancing Back

Losing a friendship while attempting to win an argument is not a risk worth taking. Forgiveness is the "superglue" of friendship—it keeps two people bonded together, even under unspeakable amounts of stress and strain. *True Friends* are quick to forgive because they know God has already forgiven them for things they've yet to do. When in your life did someone offer true forgiveness, perhaps even before you asked for it? How did that make you feel?

_____

_____

_____

_____

_____

_____

_____

_____

_____

_____

_____

_____

Forgiving: Glimpsing Ahead

Asking for forgiveness is hard and humbling, but it leads to healing. Every once in a while, you will find yourself in a position requiring you to offer forgiveness to a *True Friend*. Use this space to write about those times and about how God's forgiveness toward you impacts the way you treat others in need of forgiveness. How does forgiving affect you, as well as your relationships?

_____

_____

_____

_____

_____

_____

_____

_____

_____

_____

_____

_____

Supporting

lending strength
through one's presence

Even When It Seems Like the Road Ahead Is Going Downhill Fast...

True Friends

Ride with You All the Way to the Bottom. (and Back)

Carry each other's burdens, and in this way you will fulfill the law of Christ.

—Galatians 6:2

Supporting: Glancing Back

When things are really going downhill, it's good to look around and see who is still beside you. *True Friends* walk life's journeys with you, reminding you that God has not forgotten you. They also offer empathy to lighten the load in the roughest of rides. When in your life did someone share your pain? What difference did it make?

_____

_____

_____

_____

_____

_____

_____

_____

_____

_____

_____

_____

Supporting: Glimpsing Ahead

You can tell when your friends are weighed down by a heavy load. Regardless of what it is, they need understanding and support. They need a *True Friend*. Use this space to write about when your friends experience particularly heavy burdens and how God enables you to support them like a *True Friend*.

_____

_____

_____

_____

_____

_____

_____

_____

_____

_____

_____

_____

Listening

being eager to hear

There Are
Times in Life
When You
Just Need
Someone
to Listen . . .

True Friends

Hear Each Other Out.

(with No Strings Attached)

*Everyone should be quick to listen, slow to speak
and slow to become angry.*

—James 1:19

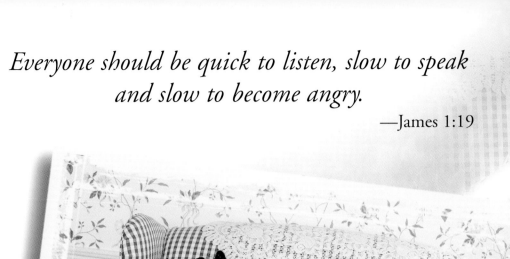

Listening: Glancing Back

True Friends know that listening is about hearing what's on the heart, not picking apart particular phrases and words. Sometimes you just need to be heard. You're not looking for suggestions or solutions, but rather the simple freedom to speak and be understood. When in your life have you needed someone to listen? How did it help to have someone hear you out?

_____

_____

_____

_____

_____

_____

_____

_____

_____

_____

_____

_____

Listening: Glimpsing Ahead

Believe it or not, a one-way conversation is not always the sign of a bad relationship. Sometimes it's the sign of a great one. Having (and being) someone who places a higher importance on listening than talking is incredibly valuable. Use this space to write about times when you need a sounding board and a *True Friend* listens without trying to have the last word. How can you become a better listener?

_____

_____

_____

_____

_____

_____

_____

_____

_____

_____

_____

_____

_____

Praying

offering up
needs toward heaven

I t's Good to
Know That
Even When
You Feel Like
You Don't
Have a Prayer ...

True Friends Lift Others' Needs Up to God.

*Pray for each other
so that you may be healed.*
—James 5:16

Praying: Glancing Back

When you feel there's nothing more you can do for someone, there's always one more thing you can do—you can pray. *True Friends* know when things get out of hand, the best thing to do is put it in the hands of God. Prayer works, even when nothing else seems to. When in your life has someone been committed to praying for you? Do you think it made a difference?

_____

_____

_____

_____

_____

_____

_____

_____

_____

_____

_____

_____

_____

Praying: Glimpsing Ahead

I t's easy to say, "I'll be praying for you," but it's far more difficult to actually follow through on it. Prayer is powerful, but it's also hard work. When your *True Friends* are in times of need, let them know you're praying. Then be sure to do it. Use this space to write down their names and needs, as well as the ways your prayers were answered.

_____

_____

_____

_____

_____

_____

_____

_____

_____

_____

_____

_____

Caring

tending to the Sick

E very So Often
You Feel a Little
under the Weather . . .

True Friends Know How to Make Each Other Feel Better.

Even though my illness was a trial to you, you did not treat me with contempt or scorn. Instead, you welcomed me as if I were an angel of God, as if I were Christ Jesus himself.

—Galatians 4:14

Caring: Glancing Back

When you're not feeling well, loads of liquids and steaming bowls of soup may offer some comfort to your body, but nothing soothes your soul like a visit from a *True Friend*. Whether you're in the hospital or home in bed, a special friend's care works wonders. When have you been sick, and a *True Friend* cared enough to visit? Did you feel better after that person left?

_____

_____

_____

_____

_____

_____

_____

_____

_____

_____

_____

_____

Caring: Glimpsing Ahead

O ffering care to a sick friend is an act of kindness and consideration; it's the way of *True Friends*. Sooner or later, you and your friends are likely to experience illness or injury. Use this space to write about how God provided the care you needed through a special person. Also make note of times God used you to provide care for a friend in a time of real need.

_____

_____

_____

_____

_____

_____

_____

_____

_____

_____

_____

Rejoicing

sharing
unspeakable happiness

Sometimes It's Hard to Contain Your Excitement...

True Friends Don't Even Try;
They Simply Celebrate Together.

Rejoice in the Lord always.
I will say it again: Rejoice!
—Philippians 4:4

Rejoicing: Glancing Back

Good times are meant to be shared with special people God puts in our lives. A truly joyful celebration is enhanced when witnessed through the eyes of—and shared in the lives of—*True Friends.* What were some of the best moments or accomplishments you celebrated with friends? How did their presence add to your happiness?

_____

_____

_____

_____

_____

_____

_____

_____

_____

_____

_____

_____

Rejoicing: Glimpsing Ahead

In the not-so-distant future, friends will probably share some happy news with you. Perhaps they will invite you to celebrate a significant milestone with them. Joining in their festivities will make their joy greater. Use this space to write about the special celebrations you experience with your *True Friends*.

Comforting

offering sympathy
and relief

When You're Hurting
and It's Hard
to Think of
the Right
Words to Say . . .

True *Friends* Know That Open Arms Say More Than Open Mouths.

Therefore, as God's chosen people, holy and dearly loved, clothe yourselves with compassion, kindness, humility, gentleness and patience.
—Colossians 3:12

Comforting: Glancing Back

Words don't always come easy. Often, your silent presence is far more comforting than any set of syllables you can conjure. When someone is in pain, being there is far more important than being able to say the right thing. When have your *True Friends* been there for you at a hard time? How did it help?

_____

_____

_____

_____

_____

_____

_____

_____

_____

_____

_____

Comforting: Glimpsing Ahead

Pain is a part of life. Nobody enjoys it, but it can be managed far more easily if you share your struggles with *True Friends*. Giving comfort helps both the receiver and the giver. Use this space to write about the times you need comfort and a *True Friend* responds, as well as the special times you comfort another.

_____

_____

_____

_____

_____

_____

_____

_____

_____

_____

_____

Inspiring

moving one
toward excellence

I t's Never Easy
to Be a Light
in the
Darkness . . .

True Friends Help Each Other Shine.

"Let your light shine before men, that they may see your good deeds and praise your Father in heaven."

—Matthew 5:16

88

Inspiring: Glancing Back

Sometimes it's tough to keep the flame of faith burning brightly. God uses *True Friends* in our lives to stir the coals in our soul and guide us toward a deeper relationship with Him. What were some times in your life when your faith was really challenged? How were you inspired by a special friend?

_____

_____

_____

_____

_____

_____

_____

_____

_____

_____

_____

Inspiring: Glimpsing Ahead

Our lives' spiritual journeys sometimes lead us through dark, shadow-filled valleys. In those low times, *True Friends* can reignite the passion in your heart for your faith. Use the space below to record your thoughts on such times when they occur, noting what touched you deeply and how you might use it in turn to inspire others.

_____

_____

_____

_____

_____

_____

_____

_____

_____

_____

_____

_____

True Friends Do All This, and So Much More.

You Are My True Friend.

I always thank God for you because of his grace given you in Christ Jesus.
—1 Corinthians 1:4

Be completely humble and gentle;
be patient, bearing with
one another in love.

—Ephesians 4:2